GENESIS CHAPTERS 1-13

STUDIES IN THIS SERIES

Available from Marshall Pickering

genesis
CHAPTERS 1—13

MARILYN KUNZ &
CATHERINE SCHELL

small group bible studies

Marshall Pickering

Marshall Morgan and Scott
Marshall Pickering
3 Beggarwood Lane, Basingstoke, Hants RG23 7LP, UK

Copyright © 1981 by Marilyn Kunz
Originally published in the US by Neighborhood Bible Studies Inc.
First published in the UK in 1987 by Marshall Morgan and Scott
Publications Ltd
Part of the Marshall Pickering Holdings Group
A subsidiary of the Zondervan Corporation

British Library CIP Data
Genesis.–(Small group Bible studies)
  1. Bible.O.T.–Genesis–Commentaries
  222′.1106   BS1235.3

  ISBN 0-551-01439-3

Printed in Great Britain by
Eyre & Spottiswoode Ltd, Portsmouth, U.K.

contents

HOW TO USE THIS DISCUSSION GUIDE

SHARING LEADERSHIP—WHY AND HOW

Each study guide in the Small Group Bible Study
series is prepared with the intention that the ordinary
adult group will by using this guide be able to rotate the
leadership of the discussion. Those who are outgoing in
personality are more likely to volunteer to lead first, but
within a few weeks it should be possible for almost
everyone to have the privilege of directing a discussion
session. Everyone, including people new to the Bible who
may not yet have committed themselves to Christ,
should take a turn in leading by asking the questions from
the study guide.

Reasons for this approach are:

(1) The discussion leader will prepare in greater
depth than the average participant.

(2) The experience of leading a study stimulates a
person to be a better participant in the discussions led by
others.

(3) Members of the group which changes discussion
leadership weekly tend to feel that the group belongs to
everyone in it. It is not "Mr. or Mrs. Smith's Bible study."

(4) The Christian who by reason of spiritual maturity
and wider knowledge of the Bible is equipped to be a
spiritual leader in the group is set free to *listen* to
everyone in the group in a way that is not possible when
leading the discussion. He (she) takes his regular turn
in leading as it comes around, but if he leads the first study
in a series he must guard against the temptation to bring

a great deal of outside knowledge and source material which would make others feel they could not possibly attempt to follow his example of leadership.

For study methods and discussion techniques refer to the first booklet in this series, *How to Start a Small Group Bible Study,* as well as to the following suggestions.

HOW TO PREPARE TO PARTICIPATE IN A STUDY USING THIS GUIDE

(1) Read through the designated sections of Genesis and Psalms daily during the week. Use them in your daily time of meditation and prayer, asking God to teach you what he has for you in these sections.

(2) Use at least two or three Bible translations in your study preparation.

(3) Take two or more of the guide questions each day and try to answer them from the passage. Use these questions as tools to dig deeper into the passage. In this way you can cover all the guide questions before the group discussion.

(4) Use the summary questions to tie together the whole chapter in your thinking.

(5) *As an alternative* to using this study in your daily quiet time, spend at least an hour in sustained study once during the week, using the above suggestions.

HOW TO PREPARE TO LEAD A STUDY

(1) Follow the above suggestions on preparing to participate in a study. Pray for wisdom and the Holy Spirit's guidance.

(2) Familiarize yourself with the study guide questions until you can rephrase them in your own words if necessary to make you comfortable using them in the discussion.

(3) If you are familiar with the questions in the guide,

you will be able to skip questions already answered by the group from discussion raised by another question. Try to get the movement of thought in the whole section for study, so that you are able to be flexible in using the questions.

(4) Pray for the ability to guide the discussion with love and understanding.

HOW TO LEAD A STUDY

(1) Begin with prayer, asking God's help in the study. You may ask another member of the group to pray if you have asked him (her) ahead of time.

(2) Have the Bible portions read aloud by the sections under which questions are grouped in the study guide. It is not necessary for everyone to read aloud, or for each to read an equal amount.

(3) Guide the group to discover what the passage says by asking the *discussion questions*. Use the suggestions from the section on "How to encourage everyone to participate."

(4) *Avoid going woodenly through the study using each and every question.* The group will often answer two or three questions in their discussion of one question. *Omit those questions already answered.* If you cannot discern the meaning of a question, don't use it, or else say to the group that you don't understand the question but they might. If they find it difficult, leave it and try to find the main point of the Bible paragraph.

(5) As the group discusses the Bible passage together, encourage each one to be honest in self-appraisal. If you are honest in your response to the Scripture, others will tend to be honest also.

(6) Allow time at the end of the discussion to answer the summary questions which help to tie the whole study together.

(7) Occasionally a discussion will require two

sessions. It is *not* recommended that you spend more than two sessions on one discussion. Each session should run from an hour to an hour and a half.

(8) Bring the discussion to a close at the end of the time allotted. As you close in prayer include one or two of the major ideas from your study as the basis of your petitions and thanksgiving.

HOW TO ENCOURAGE EVERYONE TO PARTICIPATE

(1) It is helpful to have a number of Bible translations available in the group. Encourage people to read aloud from these different translations as appropriate in the discussion. Many translations have been used in preparation of this study guide, such as the *Revised Standard Version* (RSV), *Today's English Version* (TEV), *New English Bible* (NEB), *New International Version* (NIV), *The Jerusalem Bible* (JB), and *The Living Bible* (TLB).

(2) Encourage discussion by asking several people to contribute answers to a question. "What do the rest of you think?" or "Is there anything else which could be added?" are ways of encouraging discussion.

(3) Be flexible and skip any questions which do not fit into the discussion as it progresses.

(4) Deal with irrelevant issues by suggesting that the purpose of your study is to discover what is *in the passage*. Suggest an informal chat about tangential or controversial issues after the regular study is dismissed.

(5) Receive all contributions warmly. Never bluntly reject what anyone says, even if you think the answer is incorrect. Instead ask in a friendly manner, "Where did you find that?" or "Is that actually what it says?" or "What do some of the rest of you think?" Allow the group to handle problems together.

(6) Be sure you don't talk too much as the leader. Redirect those questions which are asked you. A discussion should move in the form of an asterisk, back and forth

between members, not in the form of a fan, with the discussion always coming back to the leader. The leader is to act as moderator. As members of a group get to know each other better, the discussion will move more freely, progressing from the fan to the asterisk pattern.

(7) Don't be afraid of pauses or long silences. People need time to think about the questions and the passage. Try *never* to answer your own question—either use an alternate question or move on to another area for discussion.

(8) Watch hesitant members for an indication by facial expression or body posture that they have something to say, and then give them an encouraging nod or speak their names.

(9) Discourage too talkative members from monopolizing the discussion by specifically directing questions to others. If necessary, speak privately to the over-talkative one about the need for discussion rather than lecture in the group, and enlist his aid in encouraging all to participate.

WHAT GUIDELINES MAKE FOR AN EFFECTIVE DISCUSSION?

(1) Everyone in the group should *read the Bible passage* and, if possible, use the study guide in thoughtful *study* of the passage *before* coming to the group meeting.

(2) *Stick to the Bible passage under discussion.* Discover all that you can from the designated sections of Genesis and Psalms without moving around to other books of the Bible in cross-references unless suggested in the study guide. This means that the person new to the Bible will not be needlessly confused, and you will avoid the danger of taking portions out of context.

(3) As your group proceeds, you will *build a common frame of reference.* Within a few weeks it will be

possible for people to refer back to several chapters of Genesis and to trace lines of thought through them.

(4) *Avoid tangents.* Many different ideas will be brought to mind as you study each chapter of Genesis. If an idea is not dealt with in any detail in a particular chapter, do not let it occupy long discussion that week. Appoint a recorder in your group to make note of this and other such questions that arise from week to week. As your group moves on together, you will find some of these questions are answered in later studies.

(5) Since the threefold purpose of an inductive Bible study is to discover what the Bible portion says, what it means, and what it means in your life, your group should remember that *the Scripture account is the authority for your study.* The aim of your group should be to discover what the Bible is saying, to discover its message.

The Genesis account does not supply many of the details the reader might wish for. However, its succinct language provides far more information than a quick reading at first would indicate.

(6) *Apply to your own life what you discover in your study of Genesis and Psalms.* Much of the vitality of any group Bible discussion depends upon honest sharing on the part of different members of the group. Discoveries made in Bible study should become guides for right action in present-day life situations.

(7) *Let honesty with love be the attitude of your group toward one another.* Those who have doubts and questions should be able to voice them in the group without feeling rejected or feeling that they should cover up their true thoughts. Those committed to Jesus Christ as Lord and Savior should be free to share how this belief affects their lives (as appropriate to the section under discussion). Rather than trying to convince one another of your beliefs or disbeliefs, allow yourselves to be searched and judged by the Scriptures.

INTRODUCTION TO GENESIS 1-13, BEGINNINGS

Genesis means "beginning." Genesis, the first book of the Bible, describes the creation of the universe and of planet Earth. The beginning of plant, animal, and human life is described as well as the events that lead to a disruption of the original relationship between God and his creation.

Genesis 1-11, which could be called the Prologue of the Bible, deals with primeval history through the time of Noah and his family, survivors of the great flood that God sent upon the earth because of mankind's continued rebellion against him. After the flood there is a new beginning but the earth never regains the perfect sinlessness of Eden.

Chapters 12 and 13 begin the first act of the redemption drama describing Gods plan for dealing with the problem of sin. Abraham is introduced as the first part of God's answer, the one through whose descendants "all families of the earth shall be blessed." In the New Testament the Apostle Paul speaks of Abraham as the father of all those who believe (Rom. 4:9-12).

The selection from the Psalms included in each discussion of Genesis 1-13 describes the psalmist's reactions to situations that in some way parallel the Genesis passage. The psalmist helps us to recognize the implications for our lives of the Genesis events.

Those who wish to complete their study of the life of Abraham, or to study further in the book of Genesis, may use the study guide *Four Men of God (Abraham, Joseph, Moses, David)* in the Neighborhood Bible Studies series.

DISCUSSION ONE
GENESIS 1:1-13; PSALM 104:1-9
IN THE BEGINNING

"How did the world begin?" "Who made God?" "What was the first day like?" "What makes the darkness?" "Why am I here?" Philosophers, scientists, and four-year-old children ask this sort of question. The biblical narrative of creation is neither a philosophical treatise nor a scientific paper, but to questions about the source of everything it offers a firm answer — God the creator, the prime mover, the One before all things and before all other beings.

GENESIS 1:1-13

1. Read these verses in at least three different translations of the Bible. As you read, look for words and phrases repeated which help to divide verses 1-13 into smaller sections.

GENESIS 1:1, 2

2. Imagine that verse 1 is the only verse of the Bible you have ever read. What questions and ideas does it bring to your mind? What does verse 1 reveal about God? What does *In the beginning* suggest?

Note: Genesis does not speculate about the origin of God.

3. Look up the meaning of *beginning* and *create* in a collegiate dictionary. What do these definitions add to your understanding of verse 1? See also Hebrews 11:3.

Note: *Create,* the Hebrew word *bara,* appears in this chapter only in verses 1, 21, and 27. In 1:1, God brings into being something which has had no previous existence.

4. Describe the situation of the earth in the transitional phase in creation seen in verse 2. Read verses 1, 2 in RSV, TEV, NEB, NIV, JB, noting also the alternate translations in the footnotes of each version.

GENESIS 1:3-5

5. List the verbs that reveal what God says and does. As a result of God's actions, how is the situation described in verse 5 different from that in verse 2?

6. What is the first thing named in creation? What basis do you see here for the Jewish tradition of beginning each new day at sundown?

7. What purposes can an awareness of time serve in our lives? See Psalm 90:12.

GENESIS 1:6-8

8. What three verbs in verses 3-5 are found again here to describe what happens on the second day? What is *separated?*

Note: The Hebrew word for *firmament* can also be translated *expanse, vault,* or *dome.* A contemporary word might be *space.* Read verses 6-8 again using these different words.

9. What does it mean in your life that God is Creator, Maker of time, Evaluator, Boundary Setter, and Namer?

GENESIS 1:9-13

10. Describe the events of the third day. What new names are given? What use does God make of the dry land? What pattern for propagation of plants and trees is established?

11. What do you think would happen on an earth in which there were no reliable laws of growth? The next

time you plant a seed, pause and consider that you are performing an act of faith in the reliability of God's plan described in verse 11.

12. Close your eyes and imagine that you are a witness to the events in verses 11 and 12. Describe what you hear, see, smell, taste, and feel.

13. In verses 4, 10, 12, what pleases God? What connection do you see between these particular things?

PSALM 104:1-9

14. Read these verses as a poetic commentary on Genesis 1:1-13. As the psalmist considers God's creation, what is his personal response to the Creator?

15. Which things that the Lord has done does the psalmist particularly recall? Note which verses of this psalm seem to relate to the different days of creation in Genesis 1:1-13.

16. Of what is the psalmist confident (verses 5, 9)?

Summary

1. List all the things stated or implied about God in the passages considered thus far in this study.

2. Troubled people sometimes speak of their lives in terms similar to those describing the earth in verse 2. What difference could the presence of the God who is revealed in this chapter make in their lives?

3. What response is appropriate when one begins to realize who the God of Genesis is? How does he differ from anyone or anything else that people might worship?

4. To close your study, read aloud Isaiah 40:18-31 for the prophet's comments on the greatness of God, and the practical implications for those who believe in him. Use this as the basis of your closing prayer.

NOTES

The first section of Genesis (1:1-13) has revealed one God who existed before the universe which he created, and who exists above and beyond the universe and any other beings. At God's word of command on the first day, light appears and night is divided from day. On the second day, the water above the sky is separated from the water below it. On the third day, the water below the sky is gathered into the seas, dry land appears and the earth begins to produce seed-bearing plants and fruit-bearing trees. Order is brought out of seeming chaos.

GENESIS 1:14-31

1. Read through these verses, noting the repetition of words and phrases that divide this portion of the chapter into smaller sections.

GENESIS 1:14-19

2. What is the plan God reveals in this section? How does he carry it out? What are his purposes for the sun, moon, and stars?

3. With what statement does verse 15 conclude? Trace the use of this phrase in verses 7, 9, 11, 15, 24? What statement does it always follow?

How does this affect your attitude toward any promises or warnings God may give in the Scripture?

4. Compare the events of day four with those of day one. How do they differ? What happened on the second

19

day that was necessary to God's purposes for the fourth day? What are the *two great lights?*

5. What does the purposefulness evident in creation indicate about the Creator? about his creation?

GENESIS 1:20-23

6. Find the different "firsts" in this section.

7. Compare verse 21 with verse 1. Why do you think the word *create* (Hebrew, *bara*) is used only in these two verses thus far? Consider the importance and the extent of what these verses describe.

8. What relationship do you observe between the second day of creation and the fifth day?

9. What is God's first command given to living creatures? Consider the new element that appears when the living God gives a command to his living creatures.

10. What is significant about the fact that God's first command to living creatures is called a blessing? How do you view God's commands? Why?

GENESIS 1:24, 25

11. What is the setting for God's next command? How did the accomplishments of the third day prepare for this day's events? What categories of animal life are described?

12. Trace the expression *according to* or *after its kind* in verses 11-25. Imagine some of the chaotic results that might occur if this principle were not in the plan of God. How do botanists and zoologists today benefit in their work because of the orderliness of God's creation?

GENESIS 1:26-31

13. What two major differences do you observe between what God intends in verse 26 and what took place on the other days of creation?

14. What connection do you see between the concept of having dominion (ruling over) other creatures, and being in the image of God? Over what, specifically, is man (male and female) to have dominion? What are the responsibilities inherent in having authority?

15. Note carefully the differences between verse 22 and verse 28. Who is addressed and what is said?

16. What patterns for proper exercise of authority do you observe from the ways in which God exercises his rule in this chapter?

17. What are the commands and provisions of this first communication between God and human beings (verses 28-30)? For what purpose is man to increase in number?

18. What is man (male and female) to bring under control and be in charge of? What has man been given for food? What are beasts, birds, and creeping things to eat?

19. Today there is increasing concern for pollution control, clean air and water, preservation of endangered species, conservation of natural resources, and a balanced ecology. How does obedience to God's command in verse 28 relate to these issues?

20. Consider what happens when God's command to human beings to bring under control and rule over the earth and its birds, fish, and land animals, is applied instead to domination of one another.

PSALM 104:1, 10-31

21. Which verses of this psalm relate to the different days of creation in Genesis 1:14-31?

22. List all the benefits the psalmist recognizes as coming from God the Creator-Sustainer. How do these provisions from God affect your life? In what ways can you acknowledge God's good provisions in your life?

23. Describe a picture you might paint of any one of verses 16-31.

Summary

1. Read Psalm 104:24 as the psalmist's summation of Genesis 1. Review briefly the creative acts of God in Genesis 1:1-31.

2. What is God's consistent evaluation of his created works (verses 4, 10, 12, 18, 21, 25)? What additional emphasis is given in verse 31? Compare Psalm 104:31.

3. In Genesis 1:29 the word *you* appears for the first time. *I give you* establishes a unique relationship between God and the persons created in his image. There is a special level of response between persons that is not possible between other creatures and the Creator. What is your response to God the Creator as a result of this study?

NOTES

"God saw all that he had made, and it was very good. . . . Thus the heavens and the earth were completed in all their vast array" (1:31 — 2:1, NIV). Genesis 1 has briefly described the events of creation in a framework of six days. At God's command, sun, moon, and stars mark the seasons. The earth's waters teem with living creatures, and birds fly above the earth. Cattle, reptiles, and wild beasts inhabit the dry land. Man, male and female, created in God's image and likeness, is blessed with the responsibility of ruling over the earth and its creatures. Now chapter 2 focuses in greater detail on the creation of mankind.

GENESIS 2:1-3

1. How does the seventh day differ from the first six days of creation? Why does God bless it and set it apart as special?

2. What statement ending the description of each day (1:5, 8, 13, 19, 23, 31) is not found in the description of the seventh day? What does this omission suggest?

3. With 2:2, 3 compare Exodus 20:8-11 for God's command to his people based on his own example. Many people become mentally or physically ill because they fail to follow God's example of working six days and resting the seventh. Some work all the time, and others work hardly at all. Into which category are you more likely to fit?

25

GENESIS 2:4-14

Note: The Hebrew word used for *God* from Genesis 1:1 to 2:3 is *elohim*. In 2:4, *yahweh elohim* translated *LORD God* is used through chapter 3. In 4:1, the word *yahweh*, LORD, is used alone for the first time.

4. Compare 2:4 with 5:1, 6:9, 10:1, 11:10, and 27. Notice the type of statement which introduces in each case a major section of Genesis, the book of beginnings.

5. What further details of the creation described in chapter one are given in verses 4-7? How does the creation of man differ from that of the animals? What are the two basic elements used in the creation of man?

6. Describe how you would paint a picture of Eden, including all that is stated here. What two aspects of human need does the Lord take into account (verse 9a)? Besides the fruit trees, what other trees are in Eden?

7. What further benefits of Eden's location are suggested in verses 10-14?

GENESIS 2:15-17

8. Travel posters advertising a "paradise" usually emphasize good weather, no work or responsibilities, and nothing to hinder one from having "fun." If you were to make a travel poster for *Eden*, what responsibilities and rules would you have to mention?

9. Genesis is full of "firsts." What firsts do you observe in verses 16 and 17? What freedom and what restriction is stated? What opportunities does the prohibition in verse 17 provide in the relationship between God and man? What clear warning accompanies the restriction?

GENESIS 2:18-25

10. Compare the information about the creation of the birds and animals and of man given in this section with

that given in 1:21-30. What is God's attitude toward man? his intention for man?

11. What does *the man* lack when he is alone (verses 18-20)? What dual purpose does God have in the parade of living creatures before the man?

12. What connection do you see between ruling over the birds and land creatures (1:28) and naming them (2:19)? What does naming necessarily involve?

13. Why, do you think, does none of the living creatures meet the man's need for a helper?

Note: *Helper* (verse 18) does not suggest an inferior. (God is called our *helper* in Psalms 54:4; 118:6.)

14. Compare the creation of man (verse 7) and of woman (verses 21, 22). In verse 23 what does *the man* recognize about the companion the LORD God has made for him? What material is used for the man? the woman? How does this eliminate any reason for either male or female to feel superior to the other?

15. What reason is given for the unity of marriage between a man and woman? What do verses 24 and 25 reveal about the quality and the closeness of the relationship between husband and wife?

PSALM 8

16. Although the psalmist wrote long after the first man and woman were created, how does he express the wonder and the paradox which every human being must sense when he/she thinks about man in relation to the Creator?

17. What particular observations stimulate the psalmist's questions in verse 4? What does he understand God's attitude toward human beings to be?

18. Compare verses 5-8 with Genesis 1:27, 28 and 2:15. What responsibilities and opportunities has God granted mankind from the beginning?

19. In verses 1 and 9, what is the psalmist's response to

God as he thinks about man's place in the scheme of creation? Can you join him in this response?

Summary

1. Summarize the additional information about creation given in chapter 2. What is the major focus of this chapter? How do the two accounts of the creation of mankind complement each other?

2. In what terms is the issue of good and evil introduced for the first time?

NOTES

The events of chapter 3 are set in the Garden of Eden where the LORD God has provided for man's every need. Adam and Eve are free to eat of any tree in the garden except the tree of the knowledge of good and evil. Only this tree is forbidden to them with the warning, "On the day you eat of it you shall most surely die" (JB).

GENESIS 3:1-5

1. How is the serpent described? Compare with Revelation 12:9; 20:2. What clues indicate that these verses refer to the same being?

2. Read aloud the dialog between the woman and the serpent.

3. What exactly is the serpent's question to the woman? How does it illustrate his subtlety and cunning? Why is a question stated in the extreme particularly challenging? (e.g. "You mean that your parents don't want you to have any fun?")

4. How is God's authority being undermined and his wisdom challenged by the inference of the serpent's question? How does the woman respond? Comparing her answer with 2:9, 16, 17, what has been added?

5. Discuss the "first" that occurs in verses 4 and 5. What does the serpent suggest is God's motivation in forbidding the man and woman to eat of the fruit of the tree in question?

6. What choices does the woman have at this point?

What is the basic theological question revealed here that every human being must face? If you had been the one talking with the serpent, what factors would you have considered before coming to a decision?

7. What does the fact that the woman has this freedom of choice reveal about God the Creator?

8. After flatly contradicting God's statement, what argument does the serpent use to persuade the woman? Compare the serpent's promise with God's warning (2:16, 17).

9. What does the serpent imply regarding God's care and provision for humanity? Compare the motivation the serpent seems to impute to God with God's intentions expressed in 1:26-28.

GENESIS 3:6, 7

10. At this point, to what is the woman's attention drawn? What three things motivate her decision? How do you know that hunger cannot be one? How does she interpret the serpent's statement in verse 5?

11. In your own words, state from verse 6 what you think the woman would say are her reasons for what she does. Give some examples of similar rationalizations from your own life.

12. Compare verse 6b with 2:16, 17. What choices does the man face? What is his decision?

13. What are the immediate results of their disobedience? Discuss the spiritual, psychological, and physical changes which take place. What aspects of freedom are forfeited?

14. How does this event affect you? See Romans 5:12.

15. What do you think are some of the frustrations the man and the woman experience in verse 7b? What emotions have you experienced in trying to cover up the results of disobedience to God?

16. What advice does the psalmist give? What does *the fear of the Lord (reverence for the Lord)* mean to you?

17. What part did speaking evil and deceit play in what happened in Genesis 3? What does it mean to you to *depart (turn) from evil?* to *do good?* How can you *seek peace?*

18. How can verses 15-18 be both a warning and a comfort to you in time of temptation?

Summary

1. In contrast with Genesis 1 where each step in creation is pronounced good, how does evil enter the human scene?

2. From your study of Genesis 3:1-7, how would you define the sin of the first man and woman? Sin in Eden was not caused by poverty, lack of advantages, or by a poor environment. What was the reason for evil entering the world?

3. What do you understand to be your responsibility when you are tempted?

Rebelling against God's expressed command not to eat the fruit of the tree of knowledge of good and evil, the woman and the man commit the sin of pride. Refusing to recognize their status as created beings, they declare moral independence from God and claim the privilege God reserved for himself, the power to decide what is good and what is evil and to act accordingly. Aware now of nakedness, they cover themselves with aprons of fig leaves.

GENESIS 3:8-13

1. Review the events of verses 1-7. What are your reactions to this first act of rebellion against God?

2. There is a certain universality in children's games around the world because they express basic aspects of the human condition. Describe the emotions that you imagine are involved in the first experience of "hide-and-seek" (verses 8, 9).

3. The man and woman hide from God among the trees. How does God respond to this? In what ways and in what places do people today try to hide from God?

4. How would you answer God's question to the man? What are the ramifications of this question?

5. How does the man answer? What causes these human beings their first experience of fear? Compare with 2:25. What change has taken place? When do you think they begin to be afraid?

6. Describe the difference between the fear which results from recognizing the enormity of one's deed and the fear of getting caught.

7. Ask someone to read aloud the first question in verse 11, directing it to each of two or three people in the group in turn. Ask them to share the emotions and thoughts they have when this question is directed to them.

8. Repeat the process, this time using the second question in verse 11, asking other individuals to answer this question and to describe their emotions about it.

9. Give an example of human parents using this pattern, moving from questions about the result to questions about the cause, when children have disobeyed with disastrous results.

10. How does the man answer God's questions? What "first" do you observe here? What further tactic does the man employ by using the phrase *whom you gave to be with me?*

11. Compare God's questions to the man and his question to the woman. What differences do you observe?

12. Compare the woman's answer with that of the man. What is each doing? (Note that neither one pleads ignorance of God's command.) How has each badly influenced the other? How do the people you live with influence your relationship to God?

GENESIS 3:14-20

13. With whom does God end his questioning? Upon whom does he pronounce sentence first? Why do you think God does not question the serpent?

14. What happens to the serpent? What is appropriate about its sentence? See also Romans 16:20. What will be the future relationship between the woman, the serpent, and the offspring of each?

Note: Verse 15 contains the first hint of salvation and man's ultimate victory over the serpent (the devil). Compare Galatians 4:4; 1 John 3:8; 1 Corinthians 15:20-26.

15. What results does God predict for the woman? for the man? Though the man and the woman are not cursed, what is cursed?

16. Compare verse 19 with 2:16, 17; 3:4. In what ceremony today is 3:19b quoted?

17. What does verse 17 indicate as to whose voice and commands should be obeyed above all others? How may this put some people in conflict even with their own families? How can one be sure something is God's command?

18. Until verse 20, Adam is referred to as *the man (the adam)* and his wife as *the woman*. What is the meaning of the name Adam gives to his wife?

GENESIS 3:21-24

19. What two provisions does God make for Adam and Eve in verses 21-24? What connection between disobedience and death does God's action in verse 21 suggest? What do God's actions reveal about his continued care and concern for Adam and Eve?

20. Why are the man and the woman driven out of Eden?

Note: *Eden* means "delight." John Milton in his poem *Paradise Lost* describes their departure from the garden:

Some natural tears they dropped,
    but wiped them soon;
The world was all before them, where to choose
Their place of rest, and Providence their guide.
They, hand in hand, with wand'ring steps and slow,
Through Eden took their solitary way.

37

21. How are Adam and Eve prevented from returning to Eden? From what are they permanently cut off? Why?

PSALM 139:1-12

22. Like the man and the woman in Genesis 3, the psalmist tries to hide from God. How does he describe the frustrations of trying to hide from God? What specific places does he mention? What does he find in each case? Why does he fail to escape?

23. Children who play hide-and-seek are ambivalent in their feelings. They want to hide, but it is no fun to hide for a long time if no one searches for them or if no one eventually finds them. By what knowledge is the psalmist comforted?

Summary

1. List all the separations you see in Genesis 3 which result from disobeying God. How do these separations continue today?

2. List all the "firsts" you see in Genesis 3, noting especially verses 4, 6, 7, 10, 12, 14, 17, 19, 20, 21, 23, and 24.

3. Of the concepts discussed in today's study, which is the most significant to you at this point? Why?

NOTES

DISCUSSION SIX
GENESIS 4; PSALM 51:1-12
MURDER

The Garden of Eden in its perfection has been left behind. Adam and Eve have been barred from *the way to the tree of life*. Further consequences of their act of rebellion against God are seen in today's study.

GENESIS 4:1-7

1. Read this section in at least three different translations. Although Adam and Eve have been driven out of the garden, what indicates that they are aware that the Lord is still with them?

2. How, do you think, does life for Abel and Cain differ from the life their parents enjoyed in Eden? See also 3:17b-19. Adults often tell their children about the "good old days." In the case of Adam and Eve, why would it not be an exaggeration?

3. What new element in the relationship between mankind and God has developed since Eden (verses 3, 4)? Why is bringing an offering to God an appropriate thing to do? Where does each get his offering? What would such offerings symbolize?

Think about what your own resources are, and what it means to offer a portion from them to God.

4. What evidence is there that God's response is not necessarily based upon what is offered so much as upon the attitude of the one presenting it? (See also Mark 12:41-44; Matthew 6:2-4.) What does Hebrews 11:4 emphasize about Abel's offering?

5. How does Cain react when the Lord does not look

41

with favor upon him and his offering? How does the
Lord reason with Cain? What is the basis for acceptance by
the Lord? (Read verses 6 and 7 in NIV, TEV.)

6. What are the choices laid before Cain (verse 7)?
What is the predicted result of each? In this first
mention of *sin* in the Bible, how is it described? What
struggle is suggested?

7. Choices have consequences. The Lord warned Cain
that certain choices would bring him into confrontation
with a beast ready to spring at him. What could Cain's
mother tell him about her own experience with
temptation which came to her in the guise of a beast?

8. How does the Lord encourage Cain? Compare verse 7
with 1 Corinthians 10:13. What encouragement and
promise is there for us here?

9. Compare this first call to humans to overcome sin
with the Lord's promises to those who do so in the last
book of the Bible (Revelation 2:7, 11, 17, 26-28; 3:5, 12,
21).

GENESIS 4:8-16

10. What do you think is the basis of the rivalry Cain
feels toward his brother Abel? Give examples of this sort
of sibling rivalry today. See again Hebrews 11:4.

11. What facts are given about the world's first murder?
What further sin follows immediately upon murder? As
children born to the first man and woman, created by
God, what special beauty do you think Cain and Abel
may have? How is this destroyed in each?

12. Genesis records only the Lord asking, "What have
you done?" But imagine the anguish with which Adam
and Eve would ask Cain this question. Why might these
parents blame themselves?

What happens when the sin "crouching at the door"
takes over in one's life? In Cain's case, who is the master?

13. Describe God's second interview with Cain. What is the witness against Cain before the Lord? For the possible reasons behind this sentence, compare verses 2, 3 and verses 11, 12, 14.

14. Verses 14 and 17 indicate that Adam and Eve have other children not named in the Genesis account. Why, do you think, would the world's first murderer think that everyone else is likely to engage in murder, particularly against him?

15. How does the Lord, the judge who has declared his judgment, protect Cain against others punishing him? For the New Testament commands to us when we are tempted to personally avenge evil, see Romans 12:17-21.

16. Compare verse 16 with 3:23, 24. Why is Cain's punishment the more tragic? Note: *Nod* means "wandering."

17. What does 1 John 3:11-18 reveal about Cain? What does it teach about the meaning of love and hate? (If you wish to spend two sessions on this discussion, plan to divide your study at this point.)

GENESIS 4:17-26

18. Contrast Cain's building project (verse 17) with verse 12. What irony do you see in the fact that the world's first murderer is also the first to build a city?

19. Among Cain's descendants, what happens to marriage? Compare verse 19 with 2:18, 23, 24. How does the taking of two wives violate God's intention expressed in creation?

20. What diversification of occupations and talents begins among the city-dweller descendants of Cain? Though Lamech begets talented offspring, what indicates that he has some of Cain's characteristics (verses 23, 24)? Note the preservation of Cain's name in verses 22 and 24.

21. How does Lamech turn the Lord's decree about his ancestor Cain into an excuse for his own vengefulness? From what Lamech says to his wives and how he says it, what sort of man is he?

22. In spite of the death of Abel and the turning away from God by Cain and his descendants, how is the line of fellowship with God restored (verses 25, 26)? Contrast verses 16 and 26.

PSALM 51:1-12

23. King David has murdered Uriah and married his wife, Bathsheba. But David responds differently from Cain when his guilt comes to light. List each of David's petitions in verses 1-12. What does he recognize in verses 3 and 4?

24. In the case of murder or any other sin, the guilty person has a choice of how to respond, either in the pattern of Cain or of David. Cain is concerned mainly for his own skin. David cares about his relationship with God. Contrast Genesis 4:16 with Psalm 51:11. What concerns you when you have sinned?

Summary

1. What are all the "firsts" in this chapter of Genesis? What similar things are seen today?

2. How should the family resemblance between Cain and Lamech act as a warning to us? People often attribute their good health to having the right grandparents. What responsibility must we take for the moral as well as physical heritage we leave to coming generations?

3. What moral and physical practices of our current generation will help or harm future generations? What part are you taking in working to make the legacy of this generation a better one?

Some of the devastating results of Adam and Eve's disobedience to God have been clearly seen in the previous chapter. Their first son, Cain, rebellious against God, has killed his brother Abel. No longer able to gain a living from the soil, he has moved away from the vicinity of Eden. Among his descendants are evidences of polygamy and of violence.

GENESIS 5:1-32

1. Compare verses 1, 2 with 1:27, 28. What information about the creation of man is repeated? What does this suggest about the importance of these facts?

2. Compare the *likeness* in verse 1 with the reference to *likeness* and *image* in verse 3. According to Eve's comments in 4:25, what does she believe Seth to be? Why is it important to have someone in the place of Abel? What had been his relationship with God?

3. What pattern is repeated in the description of all those listed from Adam through Lamech? What exception occurs in the case of Enoch? What was different about Enoch's life? See also Hebrews 11:5, 6.

4. What does the repeated phrase *and had other sons and daughters* and the extreme longevity of the people suggest about the population of the earth by the time of Noah?

Note: The term *begat* (became the father of) can also mean "became the ancestor of," referring to persons

47

related at a distance of several generations. There is no indication that Old Testament genealogies are intended as a chronology. (Note that no attempt is made here to add up the time from Adam to Noah.)

5. What hope does Lamech voice in naming his son *Noah?* Compare with 3:17-19. What does every farmer hope for from his children?

6. How does the description of Noah differ from that of the others in this chapter? Yet, note 9:28, 29.

GENESIS 6:1-8

7. Scholars disagree on the meaning of *sons of God* (verse 2). Some think it refers to the fact that human kings named sons after gods. Others suggest that the sons of God are those in the line of Seth in contrast with those in the line of Cain. In either case, verse 2 suggests the practice of polygamy.

What change does God determine to bring about? For the meaning of verse 3, compare with verses 7, 13.

8. Describe the conditions which *the LORD saw* (verse 5). What words add to the force of the description? How do you think this wickedness and evil may have been manifested in the society in which Noah lived? Compare verses 11-13.

9. How are the conditions of our own day similar? See Matthew 24:30, 35-39 for the comparison Jesus makes between the times of Noah and a still future event?

10. Read verses 5-7 in two or three different translations. What terrible changes have taken place between 1:27-31 and 6:5-7? How do you feel when you read verse 6?

11. What does the Lord determine to do? Why? Share your reactions to the situation.

12. In this dark picture, what ray of hope is introduced in verse 8? See also Proverbs 12:2.

13. How is the righteous person described? What does he *not* do? What does he *do*?

14. In Genesis, Noah is contrasted with the evil men around him. How are the wicked described in verses 4 and 5?

15. How does verse 6 summarize the thrust of Genesis 6:1-8?

Summary

1. Consider Psalm 1 as it might relate to Enoch. How does this psalm help you to know how to *walk with God*?

2. Our world often seems all too similar to that of Noah's day. What antidote does Psalm 1:1, 2 offer to Genesis 6:5?

NOTES

DISCUSSION EIGHT
GENESIS 6:9-22; PSALM 12
THE COVENANT

Noah's genealogy is carefully listed down through the centuries from Adam through the line of Seth. The violence and evil of Noah's contemporaries grieve the Lord to the point that he is sorry he ever made them and put them on the earth.

GENESIS 6:9-16

1. Read 6:5, 11 and then verse 9. Describe Noah's character and his relationship to God in contrast to the others of his time.

2. If there is an element of cause and effect in verse 9, what do you think that it would be? Why? How have you experienced this in your own life?

3. Read verses 9-12 in two or three translations. How would Noah's character and the quality of his life affect his family? What advantages do Shem, Ham, and Japheth have? If your children live in a society similar to that of Noah's day, what advantage can you give them?

4. In verses 5, 11, 12, which words emphasize the extent to which the world of Noah's day has deviated from God's intentions in 1:26, 27, 31.

5. What plan does God share with Noah? Compare 6:3.

6. What specifications and instructions for construction does God give to Noah? Upon whom will Noah and his family have to depend for the course and destination of the ark?

Note: The word *ark* in Hebrew means "box" or "chest." With its size of 450 feet by 75 feet by 45 feet, it was not intended to be sailed, only to float.

7. Imagine that you are Noah listening to God's instructions (verses 14-16). What questions come to mind? It is interesting to note that there is no record of Noah asking "How?" or "Why?"

Consider the immensity of the task. Four men and their wives are to build something more than half the size of a present-day ocean liner. What practical details will necessarily be involved?

GENESIS 6:17-22

8. What does God reveal about how he intends to accomplish his intention of verse 13? What emotions and reactions do you think Noah might have at this point?

9. *But* can be a very important word. What are God's intentions for Noah and his family?

10. Look up *covenant* (verse 18) in a collegiate dictionary. Who is the initiator of this covenant? What actions will each party take in this agreement?

Note: This is the first time *covenant* is mentioned in the Bible.

11. What three major tasks does Noah have to accomplish before the flood? What words and phrases are repeated in verses 19-21? What does this indicate?

See also 2 Peter 2:5 for what Noah does during the time preceding the flood.

12. According to verse 21, what will the Noah family and the birds and animals eat? What clearly will they not eat? Why? See also 1:29, 30.

13. What is Noah's response to what God has told him? With verse 22, see also Hebrews 11:7.

14. Contrast Noah's response with that of Moses in Exodus 3:11, 13; 4:1, 10, 13. What excuses could Noah legitimately pose? Though you may not be called upon to do a task equivalent to that of Noah or of Moses, how

do you respond to the tasks and commands the Lord gives you?

PSALM 12

15. What is the situation in which the psalmist calls for help (verses 1, 2, 8)? What connection is there between what has disappeared in verse 1 and the things that are going on in verse 2?

16. What is the nature of the lies in verse 2? Where do you see this today? When "everyone is doing it" as in the situation in Noah's day, what pressure is there to conform?

17. A *double heart* is mentioned in the RSV and NEB translations for *deceive* or *deception* in verse 2. What is wrong about *flattery* and *boasting*? What violence do they do? Compare verses 3, 4 with Genesis 6:11.

18. What is the intention of the flatterer and the boaster? What does the psalmist ask the Lord to do to them? How is his prayer answered in verse 5?

19. For whom is the Lord concerned?

20. In contrast to the words of the flatterer and the deceiver, to what are the words of the Lord compared? In response to this, what is the psalmist's closing prayer?

Summary

1. Compare Genesis 6:8, 9, 22. What connection do you think there is between obedience and God's favor?

2. Consider how Noah made the difference between the survival and the destruction of mankind. What does it mean in your life to walk with God?

NOTES

Because all the people had become evil and corrupt and the earth was full of violence, God determined to destroy mankind. He instructed Noah to construct a boat or ark into which he and his family are to bring a certain number of every kind of bird and animal, and a store of food sufficient for all.

GENESIS 7:1-16

1. Why are Noah and his household the only ones to enter the ark? What specific instructions does Noah receive (verses 1-4)? What problems and complications could be involved in this embarkation? What time pressure are they under? (People who have had to travel with even a dog and cat can imagine some of the problems the Noah family faced.)

2. Compare 6:22; 7:5, 9, 16. What pattern do you observe in Noah's life? Consider the difficulty of some of the things Noah has been told to do (6:14-16, 19-21; 7:2, 3). What sort of planning and preparation as well as physical labor would be involved in all of this?

3. What is the date of the beginning of the flood related to? What happens on that day? Where does the water come from?

4. What impact does the repetition in more detail of who entered the ark (verses 13-16) give to the account?

5. Considering what will happen to those outside the ark, what is significant about who closes the door? If you were writing a symphony on the life of Noah, how

would you orchestrate the music for *"Then the LORD shut him in"*?

6. To what still future event does Jesus later compare the flood in Noah's day? See Matthew 24:36-44. What similarities does he point out between the two events? What command is given to all who follow Jesus?

GENESIS 7:17-24

7. What details are given about the flood (verses 17-20) from the perspective of those in the ark? Describe the results of the flood (verses 21-24). What words do you find particularly poignant? Why?

8. Review the reasons for this great tragedy.

9. At what points would Noah have cause to be thankful that the ark is not his invention, and that he has followed the Lord's instructions carefully? When have you been comforted by the knowledge that you are acting in accordance with God's word? What perspective can Noah's situation give us on the importance of day by day obedience to God's commands?

GENESIS 8:1-19

10. Describe some of the ways you think Noah and his family would be kept busy during their time in the ark? What concern might they feel as the months go by? What assurance is there in the statements of verse 1?

11. What actions does God take to end the flood? In comparison to the forty days it took the rain and subterranean waters to cause the deluge, how long does it take for the waters to recede? What stages of the receding of the waters are mentioned?

12. Try to put yourself in the place of Noah's family during this time. How would you feel when you become aware that the ark is no longer floating free? When you see the tops of the mountains?

13. What actions does Noah take (verses 6-12)? What conclusions may be drawn about what things God will do for man, what things he expects man to do for himself? How does this help you to know what to pray for in certain situations (such as in looking for a job)?

14. One scholar, tabulating the various intervals mentioned, concludes that the flood lasted 371 days. What do you think would have been the most difficult times for those in the ark? Why?

What specific strengths and weaknesses have you observed in people under pressure? Give specific illustrations.

15. At long last the time comes when the ground is dry. What are God's instructions now to Noah?

16. Note the orderliness of the exit from the ark in verses 18 and 19. How do animals which have been in captivity for an extended length of time react when they are first released? Many drawings have been done of the animals entering the ark. How would you depict their departure from the ark?

GENESIS 8:20-22

17. What is Noah's first act upon leaving the ark? What is the Lord's response? Compare verses 21, 22 with 6:5-7.

Note: The number of *clean* animals and birds taken into the ark (7:2, 3) was sufficient to allow for this sacrifice without destroying its kind from the earth.

18. By first sacrificing to the Lord, what is Noah saying about what is important in his life? about his attitude to the Lord? What other things could have been on his list of priorities at this point?

Note: Although Noah is the first person recorded in the Bible to have built an altar, many scholars think this practice predates Noah (see Gen. 4:4).

19. What comfort does God's promise in verses 21

and 22 give to those who live in troubled times when wickedness increases, or natural calamities of flood or drought occur? What would happen if we could not depend on what God promises in verse 22?

20. Upon what does this promise of God depend? Upon what does it *not* depend? What evidence of God's mercy have you seen in your life?

PSALM 93

21. Though this psalm was written long after Noah's time, read it as an expression of how Noah and his family might feel in Genesis 8:18-20 after the flood. What are your thoughts and emotions as you read verses 3 and 4?

22. Compare verses 1, 5a with Genesis 8:21, 22. How does this psalm express faith in these promises given after the flood?

Summary

What example does Noah set for us of faith and endurance expressed in obedience to the Lord?

NOTES

Their yearlong stay in the ark ended, Noah and his wife, their family, and all the pairs of birds and animals who were preserved from the devastation of the flood, have come out of the ark. The Lord has promised that he will never again curse the ground or destroy all living creatures because of man. Day and night and the cycle of the seasons will continue as long as the earth endures.

GENESIS 9:1-7

1. Compare 9:1-3 and 1:27-30. What similarities and what differences do you observe? In what ways could verses 1-3 be called a recommissioning of mankind?

2. What will be the attitude of beasts and birds toward humans? Consider how man has tamed animals which are physically stronger than himself. Why was this special protection for man not necessary at the beginning in Eden?

3. What new food law does God give, but with what restriction? See also Leviticus 17:10, 11 for the law stated later under Moses. What does the *blood* symbolize?

4. How is human life to be protected? What is the penalty for murder? Why?

5. How does the prohibition against murder suggest, while this is a new beginning for man on earth, that this is not going to be like the first beginning in Eden? What was permanently lost in the events of Genesis 3?

6. What new covenant does God establish with Noah and his descendants? Who and what is included in this covenant?

7. Describe the sign of the covenant. How is it peculiarly appropriate as a symbol of this covenant with Noah and his descendants? What is to be the function of this sign for God and for man?

Without God's promise and sign, what would be the fear whenever there was a period of unusually heavy rain?

8. In God's previous covenant with Noah (6:18 ff.), what was Noah required to do? What is required of Noah and those after him in this covenant after the flood (9:1-7)?

9. Whenever you see a rainbow in the clouds, what events and promises from Genesis will you remember?

GENESIS 9:18-28

10. What perspective do verses 18 and 19 give to the event which immediately follows? Exactly what happens in verses 20-23?

11. From 9:24, who is the youngest of the three brothers? What does a younger brother often strive for? Imagine the dialog between Ham and his brothers.

12. How is Ham's attitude and conduct dishonoring to his father? Compare Ham's attitude toward Noah's nakedness with God's attitude toward the nakedness of Adam and Eve in 3:8-11, 21.

13. As a result of this episode, what curse does Noah pronounce upon the descendants of Canaan, Ham's son? What relationships are predicted between the descendants of Noah's three sons?

14. What special blessing is pronounced for Shem? How is Japheth included?

Note: Many years later the Israelites, descendants

of Shem, dispossessed the Canaanites when they came to possess the promised land.

GENESIS 10:1-32

15. As you read this chapter, sketch on a sheet of paper the lines of descent from Noah's sons after the flood. What summary statement introduces and closes this chapter? What statement concludes the listing of each son's descendants?

16. Where do these different tribes (clans) and nations settle? What varied cultures do they develop?

Note: *Sons* in verses 2-7, 20-23, 29-31 may mean "descendants" or "successors" or "nations"; *father* in verses 8, 13, 15, 24, 26 may mean "ancestor," "predecessor," or "founder."

17. In the listing of peoples and nations, details are included about a few individuals and groups. What do you learn about: Javan's descendants (verse 4, 5)? Nimrod, his kingdom and accomplishments (verses 8-12)? Shem (verse 21)? Peleg (verse 25)?

PSALM 96

18. As you read this psalm, keep in mind God's covenant after the flood with Noah and his descendants. What appropriate responses to that covenant are found in this psalm? List all the things the psalmist calls people to do.

19. What reasons are given to praise and fear the Lord? How does the Lord differ from other gods?

20. The beginnings of peoples and nations are described in Genesis 10. What does the psalmist call upon the nations to do (verses 7-10)? Of what should the nations remind one another?

21. How does the psalmist involve all of nature in praise to the Lord? What future event does the psalmist speak

of (verse 13)? How will all nations and peoples of the world be treated?

Summary

Summarize briefly the commands and promises of God to Noah and his descendants after the flood.

NOTES

NOTES

After the flood God established his covenant with Noah and his descendants, and all living creatures, promising that never again would a flood destroy all life on the earth. Blessed by God and commanded to fill the earth, the descendants of Noah migrated from the land of Ararat (near Lake Van in Armenia), spreading throughout the middle east. The incident at Babel relates to the migration of Ham's descendants in the line of Cush and Nimrod (10:8-10).

GENESIS 11:1-9

1. Read verse 1 in several translations. Then compare with 10:5b, 20, 31. What tremendous advantages are there in having one language that everyone speaks and understands?

2. What does the previous mention of Shinar (Babylonia) in 10:8-10 tell you about the people of Shinar?

3. As a group, read two times in unison the quotations in verses 3, 4, the first time in a conspiratorial way, the second in a triumphant mood. What are these people trying to achieve in building the tower? What are they trying to prevent? (Compare God's instructions to Noah and his sons, 9:1.) See also 4:16, 17 for the first city builder.

4. Compare their motivations as builders with Noah's in 8:20. For whose glory are the people of Shinar

building? Who are they worshiping? Against whom are they in rebellion?

How can we discern when we are building for the glory of God or for our own glory? Why is the latter a dangerous thing to do?

5. What does the Lord do, and why? Compare what happens (verses 8, 9) with what the people had feared (verse 4).

GENESIS 11:10-32

6. What pattern is followed in listing the genealogy in verses 10-25? Whose line does it trace? Compare briefly with the genealogy from Adam to Noah in chapter 5. What difference is there in the ages listed for fatherhood.

Note: *Father* in verses 10-25 may mean *ancestor*. This brief listing can cover thousands of years.

7. With whom does the listing of Shem's descendants stop? What facts do you learn about Terah's family and their travels? Locate Ur, Haran, and Canaan on the map on page 77.

GENESIS 12:1-9

8. When was the last time in Genesis that God is recorded as speaking directly to a human being? What does this suggest about the importance of Abram? What command is Abram given, and what promise?

10. How does the Lord identify himself with Abram? How will other people's treatment of Abram affect the way that they are treated by the Lord? For Paul's comment in the New Testament on verse 3c, see Galatians 3:6-9, especially 8 and 9.

11. Describe the details of Abram's response to God's command. What would be some of the complications involved in those days in moving that distance with that number of people? in that sort of move?

12. Read verse 7 in the context of verses 6b and 11:30. What questions might well arise in Abram's mind? Yet what is Abram's response to God's promise?

13. If Abram thought back to the experiences of his ancestor Shem who, with Noah his father, built the ark and survived the flood, how might he view God's promise? What spiritual history do you have to help you in times of new problems or new spiritual journeys?

14. How is 12:7 a working out of Noah's words in 9:24-26?

PSALM 37:1-11

15. The men of Babel were not the last to try to build empires where they could rule like gods. What is the psalmist's advice to the godly who live in a world where evil men succeed in their schemes? Why?

16. Against what possible reactions (verses 1, 7, 8) does the psalmist warn his hearers? What prescription does he give for one's attitudes and actions instead?

17. Describe each thing the Lord will do for the one who follows the psalmist's advice.

18. To what do anger, wrath, and fretting (worry) tend to lead? Why, according to this psalm, are they unnecessary?

19. How can you learn to *wait for the Lord* and *not fret?* What actions do verses 3 and 4 instruct you to take?

Summary

1. Trace the different separations ("deaths") that have occurred thus far in Genesis as a result of Adam and Eve's rebellion against God. Note 3:8-10, 12, 23, 24; 4:8, 13-16; 11:9.

2. How might Psalm 37:7-11 be a suitable summation of Genesis 11:1-9? With Genesis 12:6, 7 read Psalm 37:9.

Chapter 10 was concerned with all the descendants of Noah after the flood. In chapter 11 the Genesis account narrowed its focus to the descendants of Shem, and among them the family of Terah. Chapter 12 deals with the individual Abram and his family.

GENESIS 12:10-20

1. Review the events of 12:1-9 as background for the situation in verse 10. What fears does Abram have about going into Egypt?

Note: Sustained by the annual flooding of the Nile, Egypt would not experience the famine felt in Canaan, quickly caused by the failure of rains in that area.

2. What plan does Abram ask Sarai to follow? See 20:11-13 for how long they have had this arrangement.

3. What do you learn about Sarai's appearance from Abram and from the Egyptians? What happens to Sarai? to Abram? Why?

4. How does the Lord bring an end to Abram and Sarai's stay in Egypt? Read aloud Pharaoh's questions to Abram (verses 18, 19) as you think he might have asked them. In spite of the way Abram has acted, what evidence do you see of God's mercy? What degree of morality does Pharaoh exhibit?

5. Consider the various ways the Lord uses to move his people. Why might Abram be tempted to stay permanently in Egypt?

More than once in the Bible, Egypt becomes a haven for

God's people from which they later return to their own land. See Genesis 46:1-4; Matthew 2:13-15, 19-21.

What are the places, attitudes, situations from which you should move out?

GENESIS 13:1-13

6. After being put out of Egypt, where does Abram go? What does he do? What problem arises between Abram and Lot? How does Abram handle the situation? What do you learn about him and about Lot?

Note: *the Nageb (Negev)* — the dry region south of Beersheba stretching to the Sinai highlands.

7. For what is Abram concerned? For what is he not concerned? How do you account for his generous spirit? Why can those who trust the Lord dare to be generous?

8. Since Abram is Lot's uncle, what would be the appropriate response from Lot? What apparently influences Lot's choice? But what does the writer of Genesis observe about the people living where Lot now settles?

Upon which factors — financial, geographic, social, spiritual — do you make decisions? Share examples.

9. From the time of Cain and Abel, the Lord has judged men and women on the basis of their spiritual integrity. See 4:6, 7; 6:5, 9-11. How can you begin to develop the characteristics of Abel, Noah, and Abram, and reject the ways of Cain, the values of the society of Noah's day, and the pattern of Lot?

10. Share experiences you have had in which neighbors have affected your life for good or for ill.

GENESIS 13:14-18

11. At what point does the Lord speak again to Abram? Lot may have chosen the fertile plain of Jordan (an

oval-shaped territory around the Dead Sea), but what does the Lord promise to Abram? What does he instruct Abram to do?

Note: Verse 17 — probably a symbolic legal rite, staking one's claim to real estate.

12. Compare verses 14-17 with 12:1-3. How does God expand and make more specific his previous promise to Abram? What are the two major parts of his promise? In what graphic ways does the Lord describe his gifts?

13. What faith is required in obedience to the command in verse 17? What situation is still true at that point which affects the likelihood of what is promised in verse 16? Compare 11:30; 15:1-6.

14. What is Abram's response to God's promises in verses 14-17? Compare 12:8; 13:4. By doing this, who is Abram saying is the God of this land?

PSALM 105:1-11

15. This psalm was written centuries after the events of Genesis 12 and 13 which you have just studied. To whom is the psalm addressed (verse 6)? What specific things are they told to do (verses 1-5)?

16. From your studies in Genesis 1-13, what deeds of the Lord can you *make known among the nations* and what *wonderful works* can you tell?

17. Read verse 4 in at least three different translations. How does participating in a Bible study help you to follow the psalmist's instructions in verses 4 and 5? What do you remember as most significant to you from your study of Genesis 1-13?

18. From verses 1-11 of this psalm, list all the things you learn about the character of God, and about his relationship with Abraham and his descendants.

Note: Abram's name was changed to Abraham in Genesis 17:5.

73

Summary

1. What examples of faith and of lack of faith do you see in today's study?

2. What examples of selfishness and of generosity are found in today's study?

3. What particular acts of God's kindness and generosity do you recall from this study series in Genesis?

Groups who wish to continue the study of Abraham's life and the remaining chapters of Genesis may use the study guide *Four Men of God (Abraham, Joseph, Moses, David)* in the Neighborhood Bible Studies series, available from this publisher.

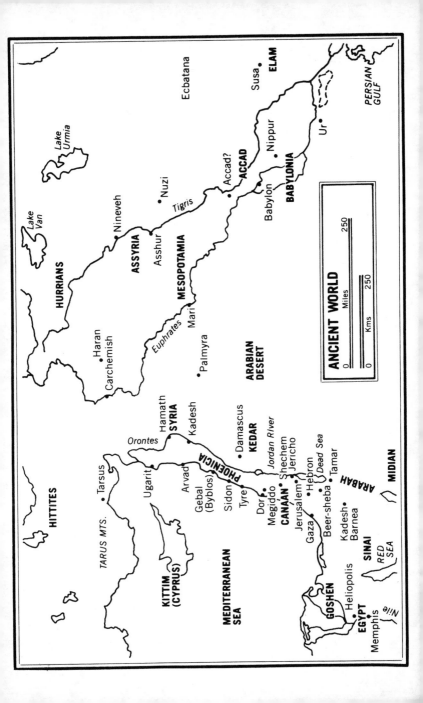

NOTES